Wearing Stripes

AND

Reading between the Lines

Amanda Michelle Johnson

This book is dedicated to
Liza June Powell Johnson.

We rise above our faults.
Then, we embrace them.
I never thought of you as my sister.
But, now, I believe.

Happenstance is not something I believe in. Alone, we are impossible beings. And, together, we relive every moment of the past experiences we have shared. Combined, we are regal extremities of the Goliath of life that hates the David of our individual souls.

Just because something sounds good doesn't mean it is. Michael Jordan retired. Paul the Apostle did not defeat the evil of the Roman Empire; he endured it. Enduring is not sympathy, uncovered, but it is sadness revealed. And, to me, that required patience. We are all entirely alone in our fears.

Happiness is not happenstance. We are going somewhere in this life, and sometimes I wonder why our society acts as though it is a journey, instead of a destination. I never saw *that* in the scriptures. *Life is a journey*, I heard often while I was married for three years, and it wasn't something I ever could swallow.

If I could not count on getting anywhere, then why in the world would I even try to get there? Who I am is important, but isn't there an end to all this crap that I see in the world? The media can't be lying to me constantly. There is a doubting Thomas in me. But, life is not all roses. I am a person. I am just a person.

I wasn't sure that I would make it far enough to write the words of my heart. My heart ached for reason during ten years of torture, and I wasn't a very happy girl because of it. I hated church, and I kept going despite the anger in my heart. I was, for all intents and purposes of this world, in contempt of the people who raised me. And following the most distinct mistakes I made, and the decisions that I was going to make, I was not taken into a supportive environment.

It's not that I didn't want to try to be a good person, but I felt so good when I was bad--if that makes sense. I wasn't confident in my abilities to keep my heart, but I knew how to be good. I wasn't sure I could make the cut for a good girl. But, I played the part. I made the sacrifices. I took the heat after a few mistakes.

I reconcile this book to the events of my past, like a zebra that knows its name but does not know how to keep out of harm's way. I chose the title based on the idea of Upton Sinclair in *The Jungle*, where he uses the term to describe the lives of immigrants in the American Revolution of men and women who wanted to keep their lives and took a risk by moving into unknown worlds of working classes.

This completely describes the inability of myself to complete my dreams in an area of the world that desires dependency on each other.

Whether independent or not, those who care not for the work they have to do and will eventually fall into derision. I chose to do the best I could with what I had, and I was accosted for the desires of my heart. My dreams are not just dreams. They are mine.

And I stand out among the rest, whether I like it or not.

To the appeasement of my predators.

The Containment of Fear

The place I lived when I was in the city of Indianapolis was a large suburban complex on the Northeastern side of Indy. I felt angry there.

Take a nineties rewind. I started high school in 1999.

I knew I was sick the moment I began my high school career. That is when I met my husband. At the time, he was a happy fourteen year-old boy. He would ask me for my number at every church dance we had. He would lose the paper or forget it, but I would always tell him again.

I remember the day that we met. It wasn't the last time I would see him, and he was leaving for Utah soon. I had been thinking about dating someone, and I bent over backwards to make him know I wanted to see him. He glanced at me, and he nodded his head as if in agreement that he would call me. I hoped that I would never have to see him alone. If I did, I knew I would be in trouble. He was glorious.

For most of my marriage, I wished for a different daily routine, not knowing that the truth of my life was waiting just beneath the surface. I was not alone at all, yet I felt it all around me: loneliness. And, when that happens, my friends, you no longer have a marriage. What was once a reconciliation of wills has become a friendly game of give and take.

Despite myself, I forgot the world and gave myself to him.

When god gave me Josh, I thought I was happier just letting myself function in the day-to-day routines. What was my fear was actually my purpose, and it perpetuated me to grief on a continual basis. I was aching for someone to take me back home to the place where my life fell apart.

Being a church goer does not preclude us from judgment, and as a woman, I often take the passenger's seat, dealing more with my feelings instead of letting them out, giving them a name, and finding my voice. Being happy is not so much about doing as it is knowing who I am.

When the father is open to change, he can mold his advice to her, allowing her to feel, giving feedback along the way, and hoping to entomb her body with his arms. It is said that we are only as good as the stock we come from, but that is was not easy for me to understand. I never have had that.

Speaking generally, we do too much, ask for very little, and die a short life without living. According to the Midwest, It breaks my heart. We don't ask for what we want.

Hating people is only appropriate when there is a need for someone to get over their love. I wanted to love a man since I can really remember. My dad left when I was two, and I found out about it long after it all happened. My whole life, I felt like there was a missing piece, and I couldn't really find out what it was, until I pushed myself to the end of my abilities, whether that was running, writing, talking, or working. I was certain that something would have to fill it. Always, there was a sense of guilt for being happy.

I hated family gatherings, and without knowing it, I would seclude myself into an adjacent room and listen for someone to say my name, so that nobody would have to wonder if I was staring at the wall. I felt that was the only way for me to maintain my sanity. I hated myself, even in those adjacent rooms, and I wanted to cry every time I left. It was an avoidant-attachment behavior.

Life is a gift. Yet, we, as adults, become distracted with who we are as people, overly confident and unaware of the power we have, so that life becomes a gypsy fest: "The more the merrier." In fact, the less we talk about the beauty in life, the more we placate our internal desires for power, and the less we recognize what is already there.

There isn't enough of the plain and ordinary women who hate themselves enough to love a man and love God.

To hate is to despise, and in my mind, that is all that I can do sometimes to make or break my day. The fact is that if I love God and love myself, there is a problem. God is a perfect being, and despite all I may do right, I know that I will eventually fail. At some future time, I will fail. And, even though I may try again, I will fail again. I am not a failure.

But, inevitably the cycle repeats itself.

Let me be clear. I'm not asking for anyone's sympathy here. I have a need to talk about these things only because I believe that we all feel isolated in one way or another. Yet, for some reason, mine was very profound. It was incredibly difficult and the dearth of good emotion that I felt was beyond real comprehension. It was a tragedy.

But, all of these tragedies have an end.

Change is the only thing we have guaranteed, and I have always fought the need to conform—to anything or anyone. That struggle brought on pain and torment because of fear. If we fear, we have certainly found a way to love ourselves, and we know very well then how we must become our true selves.

Fear everyday. We must not give up on our love, our compassion, our hope towards the love of a better world. It isn't in our souls that we find relief. It is in our hearts. I am always afraid of something.

I thought I would have to let myself fear for loving. And, our fears always will give us power, but it is how we use them that must predict our social status. We are not our own. We are our God's. We don't know what we want, until we listen to Him.

I have failed more than once, disappointed my family, and found outlets that were not the healthiest for my emotional problems. I still believe, however, in my potential to do well in this world. I just do it a little differently than most.

What am I doing wrong? I used to ask myself over and over again. I wondered where I had made the mistake of loving too much. As I grew, I felt emptiness. It was such a deep feeling, and painful. It covered everything around me. I was lost to it. I was indebted to something that happened long ago, but I couldn't tell just what. Where was I in this big mess? I hurt. But, the truth was, I was just beginning to unfold. The truth lay dormant.

I am not alone in my fight. That is the truth that most people want to hear. But, when you become so alone, and the answers are flung at you like spaghetti from a crazy Sicilian chef, you wonder why you became *you.*

You begin to think that maybe it's your character that is flawed, and that you're not trying hard enough to let go of the fears you hold onto. But, then you take one step into the darkness, and lights come on. You keep walking through it, holding onto everything you can.

Let me be literal.

I cannot wake up without wanting sex. It's so hard to just open up my eyes and wonder if somebody will be there when I'm ready. So, I decided to just go around hiding the fact that I wanted it *all the time.* The fact is that most men and women have become overwhelmed at the evidence of growing disconcertion in their marriages.

I cannot stand the least bit of discontent. It's so hard to lose someone who loved you from the beginning.

My father is not anything in my life. He never was, and when I met him, I was twenty-four years old. It may come as a surprise to some of you that I am actually able to speak about him. Trust me, I am about to have a heart attack. And, I have two hernias already from trying to explain to people how very difficult my life is everyday.

When we met, my father was sitting on the porch, smoking a cigarette, and he said three words, "God, you're beautiful."

I didn't know what to say. I just started to feel, and however hard I tried, since then, I could never not feel happy again. I promised myself on *that day* to forgive him.

And, then the hate came.

I hated myself.

All the while, I listened to the speakers in my church tell me that I wasn't enough unless I kept my hands, my feet, and my arms inside the clothes I wore everyday. I saw good men and women smile at church, and then cower over me when they started discussing the details of proper dating. It was a shameful thing to feel love for someone. Because, in my family, if the healthy woman was supposed to want sex, then she would have to forsake her heart.

In my church, we believe a lot of really great things. The hardest thing for us to do is share them, put them into action, or make them our own. It wasn't long before I got into a heady relationship with about every man I knew, but the problem was, they didn't know it. All in all, I usually knew what I wanted, and I had a really hard time accepting the truth about myself.

So, I kept going to church. And, I listened to people, and I got older and I thought about sex, but nobody ever told me what it was like. I was clueless. I thought when men and women did stuff, they did the same stuff we did in church activities.

But, I was not enough. I was not enough for these women. They had to want the man.

I was ashamed. Every time we were in the church, since age 14, I felt alone. And, every Sunday, I would listen to these people preach peace and happiness in married life based on righteousness. And, then they would take our hearts and our minds and put us in a state of determinable results: affection and love for eternity.

I had a big problem.

I hated being in relationships with an end, and so I just kept listening. Although I have a great sense of direction, I couldn't see the goal I had hoped for, and I lost sight of my conflict, and I became enmeshed with my thoughts.

To be honest, I just believe in doing well for people as much as you can. But, in the recent months, I have discovered that people will not always return to you what you give them. And, that changes the scope of my life completely.

If we are not religious, then we really have no purpose, and where does the scope of our lives become endless or "eternal"? Does it begin when we take the trash out because our mother told us to? Or does it come to those who keep a good schedule and a running tab on everything they've borrowed from their parents? And, when they pay them back, does that mean that they can get their family blessings for having a responsible and adult perspective on things?

God is not a good God.

I hate that about religion. Many churches preach goodness, and then expect blessings from doing what they are told. But, why should they give their hearts to a god that has rote blessings laid out for everyone who chooses the right? *It's not right to ignore your feelings.*

People know what they want, and most of them want a good day, a hot bath, and some good sex. We are all humans. I know that's what I want, at least.

But, when the pressure mounts, and we are expecting blessings, and we are doing our visiting teaching, reading the scriptures, giving talks, making arrangements for food, and doing family prayer, *we should not expect to be happy.*

Happiness is not a direct result of living the Gospel. It is a by-product. As an adult, I live according to the Church's teachings, always trying to improve, simply because I want to love God. God is not always going to give me what I want. In fact, I often find the most happiness in life from forsaking ourselves and living for Him.

And, it's really frustrating. So, I get angry sometimes. Actually, I get so angry that I shut people out of my life that don't really want to feel anything.

So, of course, this is very difficult, but I have learned to pray for the people that do not love god the way that I do, and I have learned to let go of my feelings by looking to Him for help in my moment of crisis.

Religion is Happenstance, Faith is Not

I sincerely believed that I was helping others by teaching them that my faith was the right way. I thought that being myself would mean that I had to be a member of the Church, and that being capable of everything that God asked would sincerely be converting all of my family, my friends, and acquaintances to my church.

Religion is not a good substitute for family. That's what I misunderstood as a child in the Mormon Church. I was a really vulnerable little girl, and when I was little, I got a lot of attention from a lot of well-meaning people. I guess this is because they were thinking of my loss, and maybe what my mom was facing. But, truth be told, I never felt like I was being patronized. I always felt true love.

What I didn't realize is that it isn't okay to just accept good gifts. After a while, I was able to learn to give too, and that was a lot better than becoming a self-conceited woman who took from others. Because, of course, in today's society, give-and-take relationships are the only ones that really mean anything. And, God is non-existent.

Thus, the well-meaning religions of the world become completely nonexistent and good marriages fall apart.

I have always been juxtaposed between two realities. The reality of sympathy for a lost father and the ever-loving mercy of a good mother, and a god that never stopped sustaining me. And, suddenly, I was involved in something so much bigger than myself that even trying my best would not be enough. Only a long, treacherous journey through hills and valleys would allow me the freedom to feel the way I needed to feel, and illuminate the reality of what was really happening in my heart. Sometimes, my life just sucked.

But, marriage was beautiful. I don't think there is anything written in the English language quite so wonderfully as the marriage vows, and I have always despised the meaning behind them. It was as if the act of sexual union became a gift that I could only have if those words were said. After all, I was only brought into this world one way. It was a defining moment for me when I took them on.

I was alone yet surrounded by people. I was scared but completely overjoyed. I was strong but the weakest of the people surrounding me. I was cloaked in determinable realities that provided an element of stability.

Nobody asked me any questions when my father left my mother. I love my mother. From the beginning of my life, I felt abandoned every time she wandered away from me. If it was to the kitchen, I followed her. If it was to the bedroom, I sought her. Despite the indignities of my childhood, I have always felt her love. I never doubted it, until I learned to obey my own voice.

Then, the problems began. I made sacrifices to make others happy, depending on my inner voice to show me the struggle. I broke promises, and I left behind the people that I once admired. I never thought to leave her. It was always a struggle for me to believe in the reality of my own worth.

My instincts told me often that I should be leaving her soon. I should hate myself more because I couldn't organize the bills, clean the linens, pick up the floor, or wash the dishes. I was, in my own right, a success. But, in her eyes, I was in complete disregard of order, according to what she understood.

It is not the feeling of hope that leaves us which makes us more able to accomplish our desires, but the act of doing those things that are required.

I learned this early on in my adolescent life. I chose to listen to myself. I had to.

My college years were filled with pain. I hated every day that I was alive. There was a still, small voice, though, that stirred my soul. It made me feel awake, but when times were hard, I felt it prompted me to move forward. I didn't want to get up and yet there was a prodding and a desire in the back of my mind that urged my heart to go forward.

Every day was a struggle. There were fifteen credit hours in each of my semesters. I remember thinking only of the people that wanted me to live, looking inside those houses, and wanting to die.

Purpose begets action. And, I will never understand why I was spared. I hated being alive those many years. I went through college in three years. I graduated with a Bachelor's degree, with good standing. I was accepted into two programs at the same time for an x-ray tech and a nuclear medicine tech. The moment that I realized, however, that I had overcome impossible odds; I decided to make myself a better person.

It was 2007, and I had learned to accept the abilities and failures in my life. I had worked for two semesters to pass a class in the workings of the body, and I had been deterred by an unacceptable grade the first time I took it.

My first instinct was to accept them.

I followed through with the job shadowing, and I made a distinct effort instead to ask as many questions as I could. I watched a Barium Swallow test, and when I did, I felt like crying inside to see the woman in the test. She barfed and threw it all up afterwards.

It just wasn't for me.

I was ready to leave the day I got there. But, for faith, I did it. The faith that I could get back to god.

I hate hospitals.

The Distant Memory

In the spring of 2007, I went to a psychologist for some emotional episodes I was having in my mother's home. I was referred to a member of the Mormon Church.

We started the conversation in a very awkward way. And, the questions were wrong, from the moment I started the sessions. And, although normal to him, being in a therapy room was peaceful for me. I was not even sure why my mom brought me. But, I conceded because he had running water machines and some background music.

Immediately, I assumed the worst. He began with the first question.

"We need to find out what exactly is going on. So, I'm going to go through a few questions. And, I want you to answer them honestly."

"Okay." I responded. *I'm sure that I will not be able to do this right.*

This was the third time I had seen him, and he wasn't all that interested in hearing my side of the story, and I just cowered in the light from the standing lamp in the corner. The auburn pillows glistened beside me and I held it in my arms. I hated my life, but I had everything I wanted. I needed help for something.

While all the people who raised me sat at home listening to the newscasters predict flooding in southern Indiana, I was wasting away in an estranged man's office, listening to the diction that he had been taught in a therapy school about five thousand miles away.

I don't know when it all happened but I suddenly realized that I was not in the middle of my best place. I hated being alone, and every time I was, I thought I would be overwhelmed with emotion. And, then I thought of the people outside my bedroom, waiting for me to be happy.

He cleared his throat. "Are you hearing voices?"

"No."

He looked at me. A look of hesitation was in his eyes. *He doesn't believe me.*

"Well, okay. Let's keep going then."

A few more questions. The therapy session was only about an hour long. But, after about ten minutes I had already lost my direction. And the words he said spit in my direction, more and more, I became less confident.

"I'm going back to the first question I asked you. Do you hear voices?"

"Well, no. I mean, sometimes, I think I hear something. It's like I kind of I need it, though. It directs me to do things. But, that's all."

"Ah. Uh-huh." He bit his lip and started writing something down on his legal pad.

Shouldn't he just be giving me a hug right now? I feel so alone. When do I find out what's wrong so I can fix it?

The breath of incredulousness gasped my next sentence. It seemed he was mesmerized. My answer was finally right.

"Great. So, you do hear voices, then? Right?" A third time.

Reluctantly, and after about only a half an hour and uninterrupted anxiety, I found myself acquiescing to his prompt.

"Yes. I do. I hear voices."

I dismissed his anxiety and sudden approval of me and looked at the old, brown carpeting, and the ancient rug with paisley in the middle that was laid out underneath the furniture. I hoped to be able to hear something or someone just want to listen to me.

But, all I was getting were less of the things I wanted. This was a game to him. And, as I realized what was happening in the room, my shoulders slouched, and I recognized the beautiful feeling in my heart.

I was finally understood! Yet, my distant heart remained locked inside my rib cage, and it pumped once to let me know I was still alive.

I looked in his eyes again. There was an absence of something inside of me. It was given to him in that moment he recognized my emotions. I wasn't my own any longer. I had been plastered to a wall of unnamed offenders, and I was not going to be the same ever again.

Remiss to Recovering and Back Up Again

From day one it was chaos, so pure and polluted with anxiety, that I felt I would never be the same woman again. So, I started to write:

I am angry now, just angry. So, freaking angry that I could drive a bus into a wall, light it on fire, and dance around it with a hula skirt on, singing chants to the god of the Hawaiian Islands. I hate my life. I hate it all. I wish I had died. I wish I had never lived to see the day when I could walk around, on my own two feet, aware of my breath, my heart, my hair, my eyes. Because, now I see what everyone wanted me to know, that I was a person of worth. I was alone, but not so anymore. I have come to meet the rising tide, to let it guide me where it wants me to go.

And, then from the recesses of my mind, as I recalled the downstairs neighbor making friends with my husband:

I am still angry. I get the feeling that the person down the hall, below the stairs, is trying to understand me, yet she has no idea who I really am. I am beautiful. That somehow is her problem! No. I am not her problem. She is her problem; she knows nothing of my beauty. Must I dress less attractive than her to know that I am a good person? Should I just hide my sexual prowess to be submissive to her needs to coddle me and ignore my burning desire to love a man?

I am a wonderful, talented, spiritual, and beautiful. How do you show respect to your mother in that situation? How do you give yourself the pat on the back when that woman is in competition for your gender rights in your family?

I was on high drive and the tension in my body was taut with an anxiety to succeed in a relationship. Any relationship. Specifically the one I would have with "another person someday" and to be "united in marriage someday" and "become a mother."

In retrospect, I remember things differently.

The end of my college career occurred in 2009. And, I realized that I would never be able to live through anything alone. I don't know when I decided that I couldn't get through life without somebody, but I remember that I was full of a longing to come to someone's side. I suppose that is why I came. It just meant that much to me to be alive.

Leaving my home in 2009 was a somersault into the cold and bitter life that I had not ever been able to anticipate. It was a feat of a thousand people, put in my path each day to get me where I wanted to go. I was failing at life.

I had been applying to jobs, as a medical assistant. I was sick. I was sick with anger. Earlier that year, I had taken a job watching a cat for a professor at the university that I was attending, and I was paying "rent" and some attention to the gray cat she had adopted.

Everything was fine until I realized that the professor had expected me to treat her as my own. I might have been able to do this, but I was not able to do it alone. Unfortunately, I wanted in the door, and she wanted out, and the agreement upon our terms was completely unnecessary. Because if I were to do anything well, it would be to impress the tenants for my next rental application. It was not a mess yet, but it was a serious disregard of my sanity. I was already crazy; who would she need to treat her kitty to a Fancy Feast? It certainly wasn't me.

I walked inside the condominium and announced myself, imitating the cat that I once had desired to keep aware.

She didn't answer.

Well, she must have taken off to the woods.

And, I suddenly felt desperate to keep the owner in the loop, so when I suddenly realized that she wasn't around, I fled to my computer, and immediately put an email up for her to read about our exploits--the cat and I.

Take into consideration that she was about five thousand miles away, overseas, and so I was left to my senses, and my incredible reputation as a responsible human being. But, the shame dug deep inside, down to the core, and I had left a commitment to mother to make it out of the house.

My stepdad required it. I was sad.

And angry.

And, then there was a terrible fear that lacked any explanation.

Because I saw what should have happened. But, then, none of this ever really *should* have happened. So, is it really what *should* have happened that I mourn? I think it is the fact that what *did* happen never should have.

Because, I hate her. I hate her. I hate her. And, suddenly, I hate me.
I hate me. I hate me. Why? Why? Why?

And, then it came out of me. The false and unexplainable experiences of my youth, and I began to think that maybe we would not be friends at all. That maybe we should be companions, and I accepted the reality of my disturbed state of mind. I was gone. All of me. I was completely gone.

The email flowed out of me, and the words gave me a relief, so I left an entire experience to chance. My life was gone otherwise, and I missed my mother. She was down the strip, the one running by the old middle school, and I decided to contact her in every spare moment I had, but I wasn't really sure that I would be able to complete the family she wanted.

I just waited and gained strength, and when I gained it back, I read the email the prof wrote me.

For so long, I had waited to know my mom, and for so long, I had given back to the church in my area, giving exceptions for the rules that I had been taught. I missed church a few times, and suddenly I was in a well-kept home hoping that somebody would rescue from the thought of losing her. I was never in as deep as I was in that moment.

I had no idea what was yet to come. So, I opened the email and read with the same fear I had experienced every day since the day

I was born. I was an abandoned child waiting for the truth to be told. I grabbed the desk, and my fingers went white.

The words went quickly from my mind into the empty core I had been feeding with frivolity from my stepfamily. I anchored myself against the desk, with my stomach touching the old, white peg-board style apparatus, and I started to try and breathe.

But, it wasn't anger that came out of me. It was tears. I thought I had tried to explain the situation to someone I could trust. I was being used by a woman, who needed a break from the small-town life, and she had been born in the country of Romania, and I realized that I was just like her.

I cried for her as she criticized the minimal effort I had put into keeping the cat corralled. Evidently, it wasn't easy for a small-town girl to move from an abandoned country into a frat town and teach at its local university. She was feeling alone just as much as me. So, I cowered from her presence and I accepted defeat.

I ruined the relationship.

Recovery 101 isn't taught in universities, but if it was, I would certainly not recommend cat-sitting.

Being Mormon

Speaking for myself, as a member of the Church, it's very easy to feel entitled to forgiveness, retribution, remission of sins, and for the feeling of security that covered practically every facet of my young life. Church is an opportunity for us to love our neighbor, yet many times, I have done it for myself. I have learned to love myself. I know that sounds selfish, and maybe it is, but I suppose it should be true for everyone. And, it took a lot of loving people who were seemingly insignificant by the world's standards, and truthfully, they still are, to teach me how to love again. But, honestly, they saved my life, and through them, I learned that to go to church is only an action, but believing that you're lost makes you want to be there for yourself.

And, I guess if that's selfish, then I would hate to be free and open with myself. Tests and trials make us stronger, if we know where we're going. And, until that moment, I didn't know where I was going. I was going to a place I had never wanted. I was supposed to live with someone in this life, and then be inheriting a rich legacy afterwards. I was really shooting for the stars.

But, I tried it. I tried being married. I wanted to die the day we came home from our honeymoon. I was not allowed to think of how hard it would be. It seemed there was a support system right beside me. And, he never left my side.

To be honest, I can't really remember anything from those first days, but I will say that I know I was being protected by an angel. Whether or not it was alive or in spirit. There was always someone there to protect me from the chaos.

The first time I walked into that door, the horrible sense of grief overwhelmed me. I was caught in grief. I was caught in a web of sticky fingers. There were in-laws that wanted to help, family that wanted to advise, and friends that thought they knew better. But, I wasn't listening. Did they really think I was going to hear them?

My heart was changing. And, I knew I loved my husband. But, what I didn't know was that I had also loved my father, and he was not coming out of his darkness anytime soon. How I hated him, and in turn, I had learned to hate myself.

For, we are so much alike. The mannerisms we have were undeniable, when I had met him that last summer.

But, the facts remain that nobody would have known what I felt that day except the angels, God, and my family. Even my husband did not know what I was experiencing, but to him, I am intertwined within the deepest reaches of my soul. And, to him, I will always be intertwined. But, it was his quick agreement to marriage that I regret. It was his undying love though, that I do not hate to embrace.

He was there for me in the worst of times, and in the end, he will only be able to account for his actions. And, whatever it may have been that he said to prove me better than the person I was when we met, were his abilities to see to the bottom of things. For, he has a great spirit. I was, and I am afraid to say it, despite the rejection I feel from him, much better now than the place I came from.

That was in January of 2012, and I haven't seen a good thing come of it since. I loved the moment I could see myself smiling from the desire to live.

Because I met him in March of the previous year, and ten months is not a long time to know that you want to spend eternity with someone. I had a funny feeling every time we were together, and it beckoned me to go forward.

Marriage had always been confusing to me. When I was five years old, my mother married my stepfather and I gained a lot of hungry relatives that made me look like I was loved. If I had asked them to tie my shoe, they would have. But, I couldn't do that. I had to be honest with myself, and I took it upon myself to hold up the banner of dignity that my father and I had lost the moment they joined hearts.

We had a terrible time getting along, and most often, I would just make it a truce between us by making sure my back was turned when I saw him wasting his time in front of the TV. I thought it would help if I could just take back what I had lost, give him a piece of my heart, and then maybe he could be my dad after all.

It never happened.

And, in the spring of 2011, I had decided that I was not even worth the back of the shoe that I bought at Nordstrom's. We didn't even talk that often, and when we did, it was like I had never even tried to be his friend, so I just gave him a second of my time when I came in after the fiasco.

He degraded me with his words. I felt angry at myself for not being able to figure out the words to say to someone who needed a break from reality. It was obvious that he had a tough childhood because even when I tried to get to the bottom of the problem in our daily lives, the mistake always lied with my inability to take distress.

Deep down, though, I knew someone was lying. I was not distressed, and I was not afraid. I was not scared of anything or anyone.

I had been in upper level classes my entire high school career, and I enrolled at a very prestigious university in the area where my Church was strong. I finally realized that I wasn't going to make it through the end of my classes, I decided to just call home, and that's when my mom encouraged me to take a break from the college life to come back and figure things out.

So, I did. But, something is wrong when the person who raised you doesn't understand your own issues and commands silence from the outside by keeping everything in its place. I felt like I would explode everyday. But, I didn't, and I managed to escape my fears by attending classes at the local university, finally graduating edgewise into a very difficult relationship with my world.

The classes were my free time.

Life at home was opening my eyes to a world of chaos, and it would be a relatively distressing reality.

Thank god for the gift of sunshine.

I had enough rain at this point.

Warping to Adulthood and Avoiding Star Trek Conventions

I am not really sure when childhood ended, but what I know is that I never got a chance to be alone. I was always with someone, expecting a visitor, or listening to chatter in the other room. I may have lived a life with a lot of company, but that is all. So, I would say I am really grateful for that, but I won't say I'm glad it all happened. It was extremely difficult to be surrounded by a group of people who expected me to be kind, happy, courteous, and smart.

And, to be truthful, I am none of those things. I used to think I was capable of being that way forever. I had a lot to learn when I got married.

Anyways. I'm not all those things. At least from society's standards.

I just needed a chance to open up to someone, and when I finally did, the wall inside of me came tumbling down, and I chose to be open to the truth about my sincere and most divulging experiences in my life, and I gave up all the peace that a little girl's heart could hold.

That day, I woke up for church and the feeling inside of me was overwhelming, and I was giving the whole Mormon thing just one more try. As I came to my feet, I realized that I had only one life to live, and so I continue to obey the silent voice in my heart that told me it was a good thing to go to the Mormon church.

When I left the complex, a serious mistake entered my mind. *What if I meet someone and they want to come over? I don't think I could handle that. It would be too difficult to see him leave.*

I pulled out in my ninety-three Oldsmobile, turning the direction that for the first time was the shortest and most efficient way to get there. I made a run for it every time I thought of having a man in my life, and I would take all kinds of detours just to avoid remembering my dad.

But, this time, it was different, and I kept my heart intact, and suddenly, I was aware of nothing more than myself in the blue, polyester seats, and I looked at my cigarette lighter, which was always unplugged so that I could get the most out of every moment.

I was a pianist, and a musician, being trained classically since I was child, and I knew that I loved anything as long as there was music to fit the theme. I had no idea how to make sound decisions, so I just kept the music up and rounded every corner with an intention to find an answer to a question I had never asked before.

What do I want?

The anger entered me once again, and my heart split open. My head started to lose its feeling, and for some reason, the sereneness I had felt when I woke up that morning was gone again. *This happens over and over again, and every time I cannot remember what happened during the episode.*

I knew I had to get to where I was going, but I wanted to leave as soon as possible.

When I pulled in the church parking lot, I felt the anger leave me, but just for a moment. I stepped up from the bucket seat and listened to the creaking door. I felt just as old as that car, but I was much older. Something was missing.

I met the church doors with an energy that I would figure something out this time. I knew I believed in God, who knew me for me, and somebody who would want me to be happy forever.

But, I didn't want to try anymore. Although, I knew I needed to keep going.

Five minutes early, as usual. I wished for something different than my current experience, and I couldn't do it. I just wanted to play that piano. I could play about a time 104 at best, according to the metronome, but I was not able to decipher the feeling I had. The beat of the song kept in rhythm with my heart, and I was not really sure when it stopped if I would be able to keep up the distance from the hallway. I wanted to dart to it.

We sat down, and the sermons began.

It was so very cold inside this chapel, and I thought my heart would freeze. But, I opened up my scriptures and tried to follow along. I was angrier with the reasons inside of me.

I thought this was supposed to work, but it isn't. It isn't working at all.

I was angrier than I had ever been, and I knew that I would have to be able to try again, and if I did, I would need a miracle. So, I got up again, and I came to the place where I had sat at the piano every week. I looked down and saw a grinning face looking back up at me, his arms placed neatly on the pew in front of him.

Although I was nervous, I looked down at him, and something settled inside of me. It was so strange to enjoy a person's company like this. We were in the same room, alone.

And, then I looked up. *Okay, not so alone.*

A smile that spoke for a hundred years would not erase the feeling in my heart, and I opened up my mouth and started singing. Suddenly, I felt like I could hear myself for the first time in weeks, and I kept going, with every particle of energy I contained in my childish heart.

The Mormon religion is a little distant from reality at times, and I spoke to him in calm tones, through the notes I played on the piano. I loved music, and I decided to stay for the duration of the meetings. I hadn't decided whether or not to be able to get to the end of the meetings, but that smile!

So, I conceded inside, and when I came down from the stand, he was turned away from me, speaking to a few other people. I didn't open my mouth. But, my heart wanted to say something--like maybe I could do well if I were able to just make him smile.

Dating was not My Favorite Time

Though I knew my place in his heart, I was too smart for him. He had "corrupted" me, and I was alone all that day wondering how I would ever get out of the mess I just made.

It wasn't his problems that I hated to admit to anyone. I wanted to feel that I was not a problem myself. So, I adopted all of them.

I took them to heart, and I left him alone to fight for our survival in the world.

He wasn't my friend. He was just my husband, and I knew how to fight for something more than the last night we had together. But, despite all that I tried to do, I could not forgive myself for those intimate nights with him.

I felt alone in his arms, and I knew that it would take a lot of good people to get rid of the past kindnesses I had accepted from the ones I loved. So, I took a leap of faith. I tried to be good, and I tried to be good for a reason. I adopted the hope that my family would be a good one, and I would teach them to love each other.

Anyways, I was a bastard child.

So, life got complicated. Really complicated after dad left. I wanted to question my upbringing, the status of my family of origin, the people who I knew as a child and all their secrets. But, as the Earth's gravity pulls on me every day, so I got crushed beneath its massive force from the beginning. My journey was excruciating, embarrassing, and even, sometimes, just wrong. I started out my journey as a young adult, hoping that against hope I would gain something more than the childhood home I had. I speak of greatness, like it were a cup of wine, filled just beneath the brim. And, while all the people who want to taste it have tasted a lot of wine before and would love to fill it, the person who is able to have it is the one who must test it first.

I will say, too, I don't drink. But, it sounded like a nice analogy. I wouldn't touch a drop. And, I don't think people usually test water as a rule. At least out of a cup.

My dreams were always set really high. I thought maybe I would someday write a book, but I never thought it would be about my own life.

I open up my life to you here just to let you know how very deflating it feels to not say much about what I have learned. It is easy for me to learn, but it is very hard for me to learn to use it. Most of the time, I intend to, but I choose to hide it, instead of being myself.

There were moments when I thought I might be a lesbian, a bisexual, and even a whore. (Because the latter is really the worst, in my opinion.) And, when I did think on those ideas, I just didn't come out all that much happier.

People really hear what they want to hear, and the truth is I wanted to have sex with everything for a because I was not encouraged to love my body for a very long time. But, I will tell you. It isn't all that very fun to use it the wrong way. People get hurt. I got hurt. And, it isn't any fun to tell someone you hate them after you do that with them. It just makes life really complicated.

In high school, everyone in my circle of friends was planning on going to college. I grew up in a small town. Nobody really ever asked any questions about themselves or their faith. Everyone pretty much knew what they were going to do with their lives. I had a best friend in high school who was regarded as frumpy, but who somehow managed to graduate and "manifest" into herself afterwards, go to nursing school, and grab the man of her dreams. He was a pothead in high school. And, despite our friendship, her physical changes made her different to him. So, I guess I'm not the only one struggling with body image.

When did we stop using that phrase anyways? I wish someone would tell me. It wasn't used very often when I was in school, but I certainly think the school system could use an overhaul, but then so could the government, and that's how they get paid.

Someone tell me when the next election is. I want to do my homework, and change something. Life should not be so complicated.

The Beginning of Faith

My family cannot seem to understand the problems they face, but somehow continue to encounter the same ones over and over again. Like my mother always said, and to quote my grandmother, *The truth will set you free, but first it will make you miserable.*

And, I wish someone would listen more often in our family. But, then, listening is always more difficult when people are screaming in your ear. And, my family doesn't understand much about being family. What they do understand is how to be miserable. The women I come from know a lot about rules but not a lot about faith.

My desire is to show them and everyone who loves truth that faith can change things. I started believing there was hope for me the moment that the diagnosis was written on records. And, all because these women obeyed the rules.

I figure there's connection somewhere, but I'm not really sure. I'm still working on it. That's why I go to church.

I have a great family, and they love me. I remember the day that the world became a reality for me. It was my first trip out of state as a child. I went to Chicago.

I walked into the middle school parking lot. It was a beautiful day in the middle of May. I was happy that I was leaving, and I was going with my favorite cousin. I enjoyed being with her more than any of my other cousins. She was closest to me in age, plus we played Barbie's together every Saturday.

This was a special day, though. We were planning on leaving to go to Chicago that same day, our eighth-grade graduation. My mom had planned the trip so that we could spend it together. She always had good plans and we made it our end-of-middle-school-dream-trip, and I was more excited than ever. She and I were inseparable. Nothing could get in our way. We were high school freshman!

I remember the day was sunny but a little cool. We drove all the way up there in my mom's dark blue Buick Century. That was a nice car, and it did the drive without dying. We were in safe hands with my mom around. ALWAYS. Never a chance that we would ever get hurt, even a broken fingernail. (That was what happened to me when I was kid. I got too many broken fingernails.)

I always knew mom would fix it. If it would be fixed it mom could do it. She was the all-knowing, all-healing fixer-upper and nobody knew best like mom knew best. She was the best person to ask for advice, and any time I made it a decision it was so that I could follow HER advice. Never my own gut, never my own thoughts, it was her advice and some select few from others, but mostly, I listened to mom.

Why?? Why did I listen to mom to nobody else? Because I was afraid. Afraid that the decisions I made were inherently bad, not worth crap or totally off-base. That was the way I saw it. I was in too deep with her opinions. I was lost in the sea of "information". She was my ship, I would steer her wherever I needed to go.

This is my calling: to relieve myself of the opinions so ardently ingrained my soul. I am a woman with a mind, and I cannot let others overpower me. Was it my choice to come here? And, if so, why in the hell would anybody in their right mind agree to something like this? I suppose the theme here was fulfilling the rational needs by confronting them with the irrational emotions that so often inundated me. It was a terrible place to be in.

I was going to steer towards some pretty big decisions in my life, and all I knew was that I wanted my mom to agree with me on it. Well, how difficult I found that would be, because for all I knew, I had been a "little girl" all my life. I was her little girl. I was always her little girl, but nothing would change that, right?

I was so wrong. I wish I had known how wrong I would be, but the current was too strong, and the waves were too high to manage. I was going with the waves, and eventually, my heart was torn in pieces by a ravaging storm that engulfed me and overtook me from the moment I realized I was in it. I haven't been the same since.

The Departure from Sanity: Leaving BYU

You need to review my first experience with chaos. We all have it. But, we don't talk about it.

I have made a lot of decisions in my life based on other's needs. I was insulated and coddled from an early age, and I really believed that I had nothing to give of myself or to others. I wanted so much to be free from the dogma my parents instilled in me. Today, though, I was going to do it. I was going to make that decision to break away.

I am determined, I thought. *I am just like her. Grandma would have done this without a second thought, and so can I.*

Today is the day I returned home from school. I have been thinking some strange things and making strange thoughts for a while now. I am not sure what is wrong. Who knows what I should be doing with my life? I can't even get a sentence out, let alone write a research paper. That's why I came home. I am determined not to let this get me down, though. I am starting from the ground up. Today.

I found myself needing something, a sense of security again after an eight-month stay in Utah. I am dreading going back there. I need somebody to help me make these decisions. I suppose it will be my mom. I get so much from talking to her. I need her so much. I went to a counselor. Nothing helped.

The day I left Provo was a bitter day. I entered in my memory as a desire to give myself back to family that broke me, but I didn't know yet how very great that moment would be to me. It felt humiliating to be back at home. After thinking on it, I have realized that much of my faith was based on rules, not on the truth.

"When do we leave for the airport?" I remember asking the uncle of a family friend. I was nervous just to be in their home. I had felt so bad those past few months, and the depression was getting worse every day.

"Anytime, the van should be here."

I sighed. What a wonderful thing. I would be happy to have it there. I wanted to get out of this place. I wanted to see home again.

"So, what are your plans?" I asked her. "For when you get home, I mean." I was so very confused, at this point, any conversation would help.

"I plan on staying for a bit and then heading down south to go to school somewhere else."

"Oh. That's good."

"Yep. What about you?"

She looked so very content to be there. I knew her history. But, I didn't know how she could wear such short skirts. They never taught me to do that in church. But, that's where I knew her from, and she somehow made it work. I was little perturbed.

"I am going back home for the summer. I'm not sure I'll ever be back. I tried to work things out at the Riviera, but I think I need to come home."

"Ah."

I always hated that answer. But, that was the first time I heard it, and so I just accepted it.

Sometimes I wish someone would tell me how to stop giving too much information. It's a bad habit I have. And, it started then, the first time I tried to open up to someone who knew my family. And, my anger was buried deep inside of me. That was the day I began to pull off the first layer of the cryptic messages that they'd sent me. It was a terrible day. It was a day I will not long forget.

By then, my thoughts were scattered, and I saw the van roll up. I hesitated to say, "I see it." But, I did because I knew that somebody would be wanting to know how to leave the situation. I mean, I did. Nobody was going to understand the depth of my pain for a very long time, and I was going to have to endure a lot. But, when it came right down to the wire, I was really, really upset about some things.

Dad had left a long time ago, and I was in a place that was a long ways from home. How I hated that day. And, I hate my memories of that place. It is now a figment of my imagination.

As I boarded the van, I knew there would not be any chance for my return.

Cleaning out the Closet or The Bathroom Where Hid My Body

Like I said, it has been a long road of self-discovery for my entire family since these brief moments in my early young adulthood, during college. It has been more and more of a challenge since that time to separate from their expectations for me.

It wasn't long into the second semester of my freshman year at college that the experiences of my childhood began to overshadow the joy and closeness I enjoyed as a young, naïve girl. I learned a lot from books before I got there, and a lot from books after I got there, but there was something missing, and I began to struggle to find it again. Suddenly, I was lost and without a friend in the world to understand my pain. I was alone and frustrated, but still holding onto the thoughts and intentions of my youth. Marry, have kids, raise a family, and make them proud. That was the goal, and if I gave up on it, my parents would never be able to forgive me. So, I just kept it inside.

Finally, one day, I let it all out. I couldn't do it anymore. I was just dying inside. It was a battle to keep our dorm clean, and we had monthly inspections from our Resident Advisor, and this time, we were not even near ready. Lauren and Emma gave themselves permission to leave every weekend to see their families. Mandy and Lauren were best friends and gave themselves permission to keep their boyfriends over until the last possible second.

I remember this last cleaning session in the middle of the winter when both Lauren and Emma chose to stick around just long enough to clean.

I saw Emma walk into our bedroom. She didn't look happy.

Not having had much conflict to deal with in my short and blissful existence, I was crushed, and took to my bedroom to sulk. She came in to ask me what was wrong. I was terribly confused with her concern because I never knew "tough love".

And, I broke down and cried.

That one look brought me to tears, because some part of me had died long ago and never had the chance to speak up.

It was the part of me that wanted to hang onto the wholeness of another life. It took me to another place, another time, when everything was bliss, nobody asked anything of me, and gave me everything I would ever want or need. I felt like a burden to everyone, nobody asked anything of me, but I was real, I was hoping someone would let me try it out, this thing, and called "life" for the first time ever. I was pleading with demons inside of me, begging for more time, a chance to make a decision, to do anything but sit in misery and feel this lonely burdensome place and ache come over me everytime I saw her.

But, I sat there, while she said, "You okay?"

"I don't know. I just can't stop crying. I don't know what's wrong with me. I miss my family, I guess. It hurts so much. Are you mad at me?"

I asked out of desperation to know if I could handle her reply. It would either crush me or uplift me. So, I held my breath.

"No. But, I think you're upset. You should probably get to the doctor or something. You seem really upset. I'll take care of the bathroom."

I just remember this ache inside. A deep and chronic ache, the same one that was there when I was a kid. It hadn't left yet. It was a burden to be with these girls, but why?

The secret was somewhere deep inside of me. If only I had been allowed to try to out, understand the truth behind my crazed emotion, sexual desires. They were beyond me. At that time, all I knew was what I was doing was the right thing. But what was really happening, I had yet to discover. It was all over that semester, but it started before that.

You see, I had a problem. I was a highly sexual being in a sexual repressive culture, family, and town, who moved to another city to make an escape to another world, where none of that hurt, and I could find peace and refuge in a way that did not ask me hard questions.

And, that was what this was all about. My body. Why did it hurt so much? Why was it so hard to feel close to these beautiful, amazing women? What was I doing that was so wrong? And why didn't they have the same problems?

The answer was in the beauty of my body. And the reason that God gave it to me. It was for enjoyment, pleasure, JUST AS WELL

AS IT WAS FOR PROGRESS AND PERFECTION. And, I didn't know it. I was afraid of it. I was scared of the whole damn thing. Questioning it. The functions. The feelings. OH my god. How did this happen to me? To this day, I question my own worth, hoping that someone will feel it for me.

The truth is though that it did. I did question my sexuality, and when those girls and I entered that apartment to be friends for a year, I knew only one thing, I was feeling things "wrong", and as far as I knew, it was my job to stop feeling them.

I turned back to her, and brought myself to tears. She had already left, doing more than her fair share of the work. What a good friend she could have been. I remember now how desperately I wanted to be her friend. She was beautiful, talented, and attractive, and best of all, not afraid to be that way. Wow, what I wanted in her, I wanted in myself. What I did, was not wrong. It was alright. It was okay. And now that I am here, I am just so grateful to say that I have made it. I am happy to be me. I am happy to be okay. I am real, I am confident. And I am a grade above those who I thought would be my friends. The people who were not real, I am confident have never found happiness.

Sunshine: Two People Together Is Worse Than Their Future Divided

When I was fourteen, I met my husband. We were young and going to the Church. I remember his smile and his kind spirit. He was always willing to dance, and he never stopped asking. I simply wanted to try any guy out as a date. We had major differences, which I realize now were strengths that would improve our relationship later. But, what struck me the first time we met was his kind heart.

We chatted on AOL Instant Messenger. I remember being engrossed by his interest in me. We talked about everything.

When I was fourteen, I was too engrossed in myself and my small, hometown life in Muncie to realize what was really happening. I had a great time in church dances. They were great opportunities to be with my friends. I loved singing to every song on the NOW! CD and all the burnt CD's that my friends made for me. I was a lovely young girl, everyone thought.

It was the summertime, and I knew I hardly knew this kid, but the more I got to know him, the better I felt. I was interesting. Someone liked me!

I remember sitting at my mom's old cathode tube monitor, glued to the screen, just waiting for the next message to pop up. And hear the quality AOL ringtone that signaled I had just been "messaged." It was a sound sweet to the ears of a young fourteen year old, and I guess I was just like every other one, except this time, I was the one getting the attention.

This summer I was supposed to get out of the house and go to a summer camp for soccer at Depauw University. I suppose it was either excitement or dread, but whenever I thought about a school activity, I felt the fear of my father's abandonment creep up on me like a centipede. It was creepy. Nothing short of it. I felt alone and confused when I arrived at the camp, and I remember wondering how I was going to survive a short week there in the freshman dorms. Everyone seemed to be happy to be there. I was just terrified.

The grass was thick and green. The air was hot with boys and girls. Both of them staying at the same place. Funny, now that I think about it. I was afraid of the thought of dating anyone without plans to join the Mormon Church, but there were plenty of good people just waiting to be heard and I was not the least of them. I guess its crazy how those things work. The best intentions would not have put me in the arms of a well-meaning man. I had to look for the way myself. And, when I found him, he would be the least likely person to have fulfilled my dreams.

Yet, I was in love with him completely.

This young man is a man of great conviction and dedication. He works for everything he has, and he knows everything there is to know. There is no stopping him. He is game-changer. Nothing gets by him, not even a good time in the car, in the kitchen, or on the bed. We were always making fun and having a great time. It was no dull time when he was near. Maybe that's why I loved him so much.

But, then I'm not all that dull, and I am not the typical catch. I made a lot of mistakes in my life, that most people in respectable society would have gaffed and told me to find someone who could have provided a safer, more hospitable environment for me to become well again in.

And, maybe they were right. I should have given more thought to the decision I was making. I had a lot to lose, it seemed, from the outside--but on the inside I was full of emotional turmoil. They were invisible tumultuous storms that rocked my body, my heart, and my soul. They kept me locked inside of a body that I hated, a heart that made a good man pass right by. And a mind that knew no reason. I was barricaded by my own desires, and tricked into believing that most of me was a mirage, one to be taken in by a helpful man, taught to deliver to him, and lose my heart again in his arms.

The only problem was that I didn't have a heart to give. I was no amiable woman. Deep down, I knew what I wanted. I wanted risk, change, success, chaos, and freedom at the end of this journey I was taking. And, I told myself that I would be happier than ever to just live the way that my mother taught me to, deprecating my talents, and hiding my love for others in the name of diplomacy. It wasn't my place, my aunt would criticize my decisions, I would be told to live in misery the rest of my life--had it not been for a good man. He was hated by my mother, and despite herself, she chose her ignorance. She gave no heed to the diplomacy she so ardently accommodated for anyone else in her life.

I married a loser. A character. A disabled freak. I think that's what he feels like. And, he doesn't like to be told anything less. And, you know what, I know why. It's because when you're told you'll never amount to anything, you get the feeling that the words mean, and they sink into your soul. They are not the truth. Yet, somehow they became that way for even the small acts of kindness I could not afford to do. The power of my shame was so great.

At this very time, he has married a crazy lunatic. A defamation character. A freak.

That would be me.

And, we are both lost to each other. But, for the record, I would like to say: it isn't my intention to be nice about this. He was my first love. My only love. And, I gave my heart and soul to him. And, he for better reasons has chosen other paths. And, for that very fact, I choose to write these things. So, that somehow, someday he will know that I have traveled the same road he has, and that he will know from my own mouth that I have married an equal.

All the incredible things he did, I remember. All the midnight help. Trips to the grocery store for some ice cream to take away the pain, all the time we spent in the shower to ease the screaming in my head and the ache in my heart, all the dinners we cooked and learned to eat together, they are the things that kept me going. They are the things that made my heart want to be better.

They are the things that in the darkest moments of my life, I would think of, and they would make me get up again for another day of terror. They would create me in a springing fountain and hope and ease the burning of a hell that knew no end.

I am not sure that this is the greatest love story ever or the worst tragedy of the known universe, but I do know that I have never felt more pain in the past four years, yet that same level of dissonance was met with equal synchronicity when our hearts met.

I am alone without him, and without him, I will remain for the eternal span of my creative years. I am alive in the years we spent together, for they made me hang onto hope. They required it of me. They gave me reason to think of myself, just for once, and I found out that thinking of me really isn't all that bad.

Exceptions to the Rule of Compassion

My experiences in school were unimaginably excruciating. It wasn't that I wanted to let someone take over my feelings, but I thought that they were going to. So, I would walk through campus, expecting to be overtaken by the emotional dissonance I felt around me. Girls were parading as women, letting boys take their bodies, and not their hearts.

I came back from school for a few months just to hold a part-time job. I was the cleaning girl on the grounds for the student center. And, I was certain that I was doing a horrible job most of the time. I was not sure that I could actually make something happen good with my life. And, I was crawling out of bed everyday, just trying to stay awake. I wasn't living with anyone my age, and although my health began to improve mentally, my body ached for someone to touch.

It wasn't easy to watch all those young kids walking into the student center and out again. It made me want to cry just to watch their bodies walk away from me. I had a desire to hug them, laugh with them, make friends, and get back at old boyfriends. So, I blew grass, and learned to use a hammer, which, ironically, put a wrench in between the devil and me.

I think my favorite part of being on campus just knew that I would be able to get exercise. It was a small campus, and that first semester was grueling. My physical health plummeted, and I would rarely be able to breathe. I wasn't able to think except when I was walking. It seemed my physical strength depended more on moving than it did on stopping.

Breathing was a joy, but when I sat down, things weren't easy, and I just stride from class to class, hoping that someone would wake up and see how much I was feeling. I nearly felt like I would burst, everyday. It wasn't my heart that was the problem, nor my mind, but my body.

Thinking of others was my primary goal, and so I attempted to reach out to others, but only to find I was very different than them. Upon returning home, one day, I remember seeing my stepfather in the house listening to Phil Collins or something that made his life make sense. I hated listening to that music. But, during a long time of influential events in my life that were financially supported by him, I chose to enjoy it.

As I chose each day, over and over to listen to terrible music, give myself to strangers in conversation, I wanted, slowly, just to stop feeling anything. I became a different person inside. I really do not remember any of the experiences I had during that time. It was difficult beyond comparison. I was constantly confronted with ugly men and women who didn't enjoy my faith.

I was beyond help, but I was encouraged to serve others at the same time. My heart, mind, and soul were torn at the seams, and I was attending classes at my church just in order to feel the love that I so desperately needed from my father. I have nothing to regret about that time. I was very determined to get my degree, and I did so.

Socially, life was a different story. It wasn't my faith that made me crazy. It was the experiences inside my doctor's office, that were done in the name of "God." I was drowning in a sea of indecision. It wasn't my life I was deciding. My stepfather never spoke to me, only talked kindly to me, watching me from the corner of his eye to see if I was still listening from the viewpoint of a cinematic volunteer. He watched movies everyday while I attended classes from early morning to evening, totaling 15 credit hours every semester. To say that I was mistreated by my family would be wrong. But, the level of trust in my home was null.

I was allowed to ask for a few things, but I never tried to because I wasn't truly even connecting to my family. They watched TV, and the presidential race for 2008 was a fiasco I will never forget. I watched the news every night, after I felt overwhelmed about the state of affairs in my own university. The fact was that I couldn't really see anything getting better at the point. But, I now realize that I was satisfying my needs for fearful indignation. I hated the candidate Mitt Romney, but I chose to keep my mouth shut, and it made listening.

Dating the Perfect Man

When I met him, I was obviously sick and distressed. I was losing hope, and fast. I knew I wanted to succeed, but as much as I tried, it never came. I had just finished my second degree, and nothing was happening. I was clamoring for a reason to keep going because nothing seemed worthwhile anymore.

We started dating, and the game was changed. I know we had chemistry, but never had anyone been so important to me like he was. He wanted to love me. I wanted to love him. But, the details seemed elusive, almost impossible.

I tried to get a job, but the job never came. When I decided to accept a position at a local doctor's office, I felt exhilarated. I knew I had nothing to lose, so I worked very hard at learning everything I could.

As time progressed, we realized we were inseparable. My life nearly fell apart because I was entirely engrossed in his affection, and I was unaware that I was even alive. I felt nothing but the need to be beside him. That was all I wanted. And, though mistaken as neediness by the people I knew the best, I ran full-fledged into it all.

It was the biggest risk I had taken yet, but I did it. I left home, I got a job, and I moved in with my family. I had expected life to be easier, at this point, but what I did not know was that our differences had yet to be uncovered.

Finally, about ten months after we met, we decided to get married. I, of course, was indecisive about the idea for most of the dating period. It did not matter, at this point, what I did. I was already bound to him completely and I could feel nothing but the attraction I had to him. I was addicted, according to my mother. Despite my best efforts, though, I had found my way into another hole, a lot like the one I had just left.

You might think I am foolish and desperate to get into something so destructive. Do not be surprised when I tell you that I come from a very different family from his. We were so engrossed into each other's problems, and that was the problem. I based our relationship on our problems. So, from the beginning, it was a match made in heaven. But, heaven seemed far away when you had so much garbage around you. We would say we loved each other and then turn around and argue. It was on and off, and I never had much peace.

When we were fighting, I felt good. I was out of my mind, at the time. But, I felt good. That was the release valve for me. I had a lot of hidden emotions about my family. My mother was involved in every part of my life, no matter how small. She knew all my goings and comings.

It had been that way growing up. I thought, "I don't belong." "I'll never belong." And, I thought, therefore I acted, and I never belonged. I was in high school as an impression of my real self. I never came out of adolescence until I met my husband. I found him at the worst time in my life, but somehow we had still made it work. It was always difficult before, but never had I felt so exhilarated by someone. He was exciting, daring, and totally unconventional. It was such a joy to just be around him. He was engaging and hilarious, and nothing I did scared him. He was into me just as much as I was into him. We met each other on the same level of intensity. It wasn't perfect, but it was a lot better than living with my parents the rest of my life, which according to the standard statistic on singles in my hometown, was a possibility. I was not about to have that happen.

The months leading up to our engagement were torture for me. I was given strict rules to obey during childhood, and to protect my virtue. I had, in my desire to leave behind my family's rigid thought-patterns, totally abandoned my sense of morality, and I found myself feeling vulnerable. I was, in the most important way, spiritually exposed and aware of all my real faults. I was angry about the loss of my father, and I had to find some comfort, and the real human side of me showed me the way. The harder I cried the more comfort I found in him.

"So, you think we should get married?"

It was the way our conversation started out a lot those days. It was a hard question to ask a bewildered and abandoned twenty five-year-old but I did it just the same.

"I want to marry you, Amanda. I think you're wonderful. I want to be with you. We don't have to go to the temple to be sealed. We'll do it later."

That was where the conflict came into my mind. How was I supposed to marry someone who didn't hold up the values that my mom held up for me from a very young age? It was hard decision. It was one we talked about a lot.

"I want to marry you too, but..." My voice trailed off. It was such a fight for me to maintain my own thoughts. The conflict between my parents and I had grown inescapable. I was losing ground with them, and I didn't want to just give into my need to be coddled and loved by them.

I wanted to be close to him, but something fought hard to surface inside of me. The need to be approved. I was hoping that Josh would have solved my need for a new life. And, so I looked at him.

I knew we already messed up and he was trying really hard to make it up to me. In the Christian world, we were unworthy in God's presence, so we would have to be married civilly. There was a big difference. The main one being that my mom would not approve.

"Just make a decision and stick to it, Amanda." He said.

I stood there.

"Well, I do love you, and I want to be with you. I have to go."

And, before I could say another word, he was out the door. It was a painful thing to see him walk out without any idea if I would see him again. It was always painful to see him go. I wanted so much to see him light up and tell a joke, make a friend, or tell me a story. But, that was what happened when you struggled with internal conflict. And, he knew it. The best thing to do was leave.

It was a few days later. I was on the phone to mom.

"I know we've been talking a lot about marriage lately. I just wanted to call you and tell you. I want to go forward with the plans."

"Oh, okay, honey. I am supporting you 100 percent. I just want you to know that."

"Thanks, mom," and I cringed to think of what she really thought of my husband-to-be. He was not the man she wanted for me, and we both disagreed on his feelings towards me. Changing your mind on your husband can be a lot of stress for the man.

"I just want to go shopping with you so we can pick out a dress. You will have to let me help you. Or do you just want me to make the decisions."

My feelings started to surge. The thought of being with her for an entire afternoon. The thought of marrying someone for the first time. Outside God's presence. What was I thinking?

"I don't care, I just want to have a marriage and be with him."

"Do you know what colors you want?"

"Yeah, blue and white. Midnight blue. I guess." I sounded so sure of myself.

"Okay. I think I can ask Dad for a couple of swaps from work. They will probably have something we can look at."

I stopped talking. I was on lunch break from work and had to be back soon.

I was deep into a depression that had snuck up on me since I was a child. What I believed at the time was that marriage would solve all my problems. I was knee-deep in the mire of grief from separation of my parents and bordering the wading pool of an infant marriage. What was keeping me from just giving up and saying "To hell with everyone?"

I think back on those days with wonder and awe. I think there is only one answer, and he is sleeping in my bed tonight. I wish I could say something made me think, "Oh no. You can't kill yourself." But, the truth is, I wanted to. And, I would have if he had not been there in my life at that time. I was drowning in a sea, sinking fast in quicksand. He was the lifeboat and the rope to my sanity. I wanted to dig into the ground, make a hole and live there, like I had my whole life, but God had bigger plans for me.

I tied a knot in that rope and held on.

"I guess I need to get back to work. I'm on lunch."

"Okay. Bye, honey."

The Big Decision

So, we decided to get married. It was true that we loved each other, but however hard I tried to look at it another way, we were in for a rocky ride. According to our spiritual leader, we were supposed to be married in a place that best suited our needs, and we decided to do that. But, there's something I didn't understand about obeying God, I had to do it out of my own free will. I had never experienced free will, up to this point in my life. Thus, the breaking of the rules.

During the wedding, I felt just the same way any other bride would feel. I was elated to become a part of someone's life, and I wanted to help him find a way through his family's problems. Then, we could be happy together. He gave me his commitment, and I would try to be the best I could be. I was doing it for him, not myself, but I soon learned that I would have to start living, instead of hoping, if I was to survive the most historic event of my life.

What I learned is that being married to help someone and being married to HELP someone are two totally different things. It differs in the amount of helping that you do. If it was to relax into a normal relationship between two people, I was sure that I would be totally gone. I was never going to be normal. I was never normal, so what was going to stop me now?

From the moment I met Josh, we were off to the races with the ideas from writing books, starting businesses, making movies, and even saving our families from destruction. We thought we could take on the world, together.

I was lost in his mind. He was totally lost in mine. I wanted so much to find the peace of reality slip into my hand, and that reality is a great reconciliation for all the pain of my past. But, how wrong I would become, I never knew, until I got there.

 I know now that I could not become his answer if it weren't for my problem. And he could not see me as his solution unless he had a problem to start with. Those were the stipulations. And, unknowingly, we took them all on, hoping without hope that we would make it somehow.

So, when I got married, things were a little like when I was a child. But, so does everyone. We all revert to our childhood behaviors, and I was definitely not a happy child. And, my husband knows that.

The important part is to learn from your mistakes. Thankfully, I always had a lot of friends to help me through it. But, moving to a new city was not my first choice on the path to becoming his wife, though I was already tied to him inextricably. Without any practical or real sense of commitment, I somehow found a job, amidst the confusion, and I enjoyed working. With whatever I had left, I met my soon-to-be husband as often as possible, since we were both working. The marriage question was left unanswered for months, which made things a little unpredictable.

Not many times in my life have I made the choice to do something for myself. I had always wanted to find another person to share my life with. I wanted to marry. And, for the same reasons that most girls do: a sweet, and lovable companion, but I had a little complication involved. Instead of just relying and leaning on my husband in time of need, I expected to engulf him in my pain and ask him to swallow it for me. That was unrealistic, and I now realize, totally impossible. I was inundated with pain, and he couldn't do a thing to stop it.

That's when my rebellion stepped in. I wanted someone to stop it, and we just had to do the best thing for us to make it stop. I had to get married to him, and do God's will. That was getting married. I could probably just have well as jumped off a cliff to save myself from an oncoming car. There was no way out. I had to give into something. I wasn't letting go of him.

I am at the writing of this book, currently working through some difficult and painful emotions surrounding that decision, but I know it was not all for nothing. I did it with the best of intentions, and though less than what some people like to call "acceptable", I did it for me, and for myself, only. It was a selfish decision for me to get married. I admit it. I fully admit that I did it for the wrong reasons. I did it to please my own needs and selfish wants; I hoped that through our union, I would be made whole.

And, in some ways, I have. I have been made more aware of the slights and intentions of others, and the issues that come from being a part of something bigger than me. I am, just like I was when I played soccer, trying to "make the cut". And if I did it then, then I can do it now.

What complicates matters is his temper and unpredictable nature, but I know through our hard work and effort, we can overcome our weaknesses and turn them into strengths. I truly believe that.

The Trip to the Counselor

They were dark and ugly. That's how I felt. I was confused by this earthquake of emotions that rocked my entire world. My emotions created a lot of space, but I wanted so much to be close to the people around me.

People who refuse the truth about themselves or others are often driven to insanity. That is what was happening to me. I lacked the understanding of an adult, and instead of reacting like a normal college student and rebelling, I felt a cataclysmic eruption inside of me. I doubted nothing in my world. I never had. I never would. But, that was about to end.

I had decided to go to school in hopes of attaining an education. I knew I wanted a good one. My mother and grandmother were both educated, and I had heard the importance of it since I was a child. I knew that it had to be somewhere safe, too. So, I chose BYU-Utah. That seemed safe enough.

In the LDS scriptures, there is verse written for anyone who is trying to make a decision for themselves. It is a story about a man who wanted to help with translating the scriptures before he was ready. He is in an interesting predicament. Although he was an intelligent man, he was given the job of assisting the translator, and he was eager to go forward with the work himself.

When he realized that this was not the proper time, God told him something very important, about making decisions. I can relate to this man especially during this time of my life:

> "Behold, you have not understood; you have supposed that I would give it unto you, when you took no thought save it was to ask me. But, behold, I say unto you, that you must study it out in your mind; then you must ask me if it be right, and if is right I will cause that your bosom shall burn within you; therefore, you shall feel that it is right. But, if it be not right, you shall have no such feelings, but you shall have a stupor of thought that shall cause you to forget the thing which is wrong; therefore, you cannot write that which is sacred save it be given you from me" (Doctrine and Covenants 9:7-9).

I realized soon after I had left for Utah that I had made a big decision, and I was eager to learn about the people around me. I was not prepared for what happened when school got underway. I was stressed, and beyond that, I was overwhelmed. I could not understand why I was burdened, but as the year dragged on, I was more and more depressed.

I was constantly on the phone with my mother, asking her for help to stay motivated, but it seemed to work backwards, the more I talked her, the more sick I became. I went to counseling. I tried drugs, but nothing good came of it. I was depressed, and there was no coming out of it. By the end of the year, I was out of my mind.

Newswriting

Nothing has more power to change a life for good than something like marriage, graduation, or sickness. I, fortunately, have been able to experience all three. It may be part of my nature, since I have experienced change so many times. However, I do believe in change, regardless of the obvious challenges.

One of my changes came early in my life. While I was attending college in Indiana at Ball State University, I was studying all of the general courses that were offered, to obtain whatever bit of experience I could, in the "real" world. As I studied and passed each class, the question of a solid major was visited often by my mother. She studied and used as much of her skills as she could to point me in the right direction. And, I listened. I followed her instruction, applying for every available program that would offer me a steady job, and a decent paycheck.

These were good and bad times. I felt so closely tied still, to my mother, but I desperately wanted freedom in the real world, away from home.

I was no stranger to achievement, but I had somehow lost the meaning of the word "success." If anybody thought I was a threat, they never said so, and I did not enjoy the competition. Although I was in a very competitive class, I shied from the idea of being valedictorian or salutatorian. The reasons for success were only to appear the best, and I was becoming more aware of my desires, not to win, but just to be myself. The honor roll was the last thing on my mind.

After I learned what was really at stake—namely, my confidence—I decided to take it easy my senior year, and I signed up for the newspaper. That was the most creative atmosphere I dared to enter, and it seemed more of a challenge than anything I tried up until then. I was in advanced chemistry the year before, but this seemed like a different challenge. I remember feeling terrified that I would say something that was wrong, or misquote a contributor, but it was all worth it in the end, and I earned Excellence in News Writing for my work there. It was a fantastic opportunity.

Marriage

I have family that used to tell me how hard marriage could be. If I asked anything about it, the answer was always, "Marry a good man." I wonder what that meant. Now I know that it meant they weren't really pleased with the husbands that they had picked and encouraged me to do better than them. I see it now as a need to reach out and make sense of their marriages.

I thought most of the time that it was an invitation to look one more time at the boys from my church, and maybe reconsider. But, I always came up with an empty hand. None of them interested me, and if they did, I was too eager to ask the wrong questions in hopes of finding out what type of man he was. That is precisely why I took so much comfort in the qualities I found in Josh.

He was different, and from the beginning, we were bound together by our commonalities. I mean, really. Our likes were similar. We both loved the gym, and we conquered every challenge that came our way. So, meeting each other and ending up marrying was never a surprise. I just wanted to make a good home, and be happy.

But, what's more, I got married. On top of it all, I got married. It was the desperate attempt I made to discover the gifts that lay inside of me. It was the riskiest thing I had ever done, and I knew it. I knew that he knew it, and we were both scared.

And, I'm still here.

Welcome to Reality

Today, I am grateful for a loving husband who wants me to be happy. I was not nearly as thrilled the first time we came home after the festivities were done. I remember waking up to an alarm, but then I set the snooze button. So when he found me wanting to sleep, I became aware of our differences. He is a morning person, and I would sleep if it killed the pain inside of me. That did not last long.

To him, marriage was an endeavor, and a union of love. I had expected it to be hard, or at least frustrating, so when the conflict came, I was ready.

I was angry about something, and if he couldn't fix it, he better darn well keep trying. There was love between us, but someone had to show it first. I was angry, frustrated, and terrorized by my past, and nobody could help me unless they stayed long enough to see me through. I was that blessed to have him there.

When I faced my demons and came out lacking, he pushed me to conquer them. That was the reason I needed him so much. We were fighting, but the fighting was the only thing that kept me going. I was still on the winning team, as long as we were together. And, even though everything was fighting against us, I found the comfort in his arms. Despite all the odds, we stayed together.

The Battle for My Life

Some people think families are flying out the window, that modern technology has threatened their existence. I agree. But, there is another threat that is coercing the family's destruction and human's most basic unit. That is success.

Though many people are claiming to have a hold on what is "right" and "wrong", there is another faction that wants to give back to the transgressor or the puritan alike. I see them both in a battle. They have been since my childhood, and they are still that way today.

My mom was a puritan of the highest and most intellectual kind. She still claims to know everything from the bottom up about medicine, books, cooking, and anything related to her field of administration. Does she get anything from knowing it, though? I say, No. She is threatened by the knowledge of others, and thus, she is threatened by their success.

There is a type of success though that is never threatened. Something that is forgiving, kind, and affectionate no matter what is taken away. That is the love of a good Father.

My father was out of the picture, and since I was a child, I knew him as a low-level, no-show type of man. When I met him for the first time, however, two years ago, I was afraid. I was afraid that he might not love me anymore, that somebody would call me crazy for having seen him in person. Everyone gave up on him, and I was the only one who wanted to see him. I was, for all intents and purposes, crazy.

Marriage has not been all that easy, but with good Father, I know I am going to conquer the pitfalls. That is why I am grateful for my Church. The most ingenious place on the planet, where people will find their faults, and bring each other up again.

This was the way that my husband and I met. We met in the Church in the small town where I grew up. It was the chance that would not come again for another lifetime. It had already in fact happened to me, but God, in His mercy, knew the way Satan tempts fate, and He gave me a clear shot at an education first. Just like mom and grandma told me to.

I knew my mother as kind and affectionate, but when my sanity was threatened again, during my first year of marriage, she changed. Her disposition towards my husband was not hard to understand, considering our violent interaction, but when I believed that there was change, she was not so eager to assume the same thing.

The reason for this was not illuminated to me, but I am now able to understand. Because of the lack of communication I had with my father, I was not aware of how hard it was to explain her actions to the general membership of my Church.

So, in her effort to escape those feelings of self-loathing and self-criticism, she used me. My birth became the reason for her redemption. Her decisions were the real reason that I was there, but if there was anything good about what had happened, it was going to be me. I was glorified in my father's absence, by the mere reason that he was absent. I was cause for their rejoicing, because she was keeping me from my pain. I was a scapegoat, and I will never be the same since I discovered that fact.

It has taken me eight long years to discover what it was that made me lose my sanity, but I finally know. I was bereaved of the right to know my father, simply because he was not available—which may or may not be a valid reason—but then, on top of that, protected from that truth so that I could become my mother's answer to her own pain. I was born out of wedlock and then asked to carry the burden of her pain for a tormented twenty five years, and met the man who would save me from that pain by the time I had reached the edge of my sanity.

Call it fate. Call it a miracle, but I am forever grateful for the gift of marriage, and I will never let anything hold me back from obtaining its blessings. I know truth when I find it. I know pain when it hits me. I am human, and the whole human race will know how my father kept me safe while my mother learned to stay away, during the most excruciating experience of my life: coming to know myself.

The Truth

I know that most people who claim to be members of the Mormon faith are surprised when they see me. I wear colorful clothes, say colorful things, and stay active outside of the Church. That may seem like hypocrisy, but for a girl who never knew the world outside her front door, it is called being a Saint. A Latter-Day Saint. I give whatever I have and let God's blessings unfold. And, they do.

That is why I have chosen to stick with it in marriage. I decided a few weeks ago that I would not let the past define my future. Josh and I both had hard decisions to make early in life. When we got married, I thought it would be different.

I think God had a big task for me when I was living with him before the earth was created. When I got the news that I would be given the task to change my family's storyline, he decided to give me a gift. Something that I could have to help me through the process. He gave me some*one*. And, he had to experience life the same way I had, with tests to determine his strength of character and his identity early in life. It was Josh.

His character has been tried as many times or more than mine, and his identity shaped by severe emotional and physical trauma. I could not be more blessed to have someone to show me the way through the pain I had experienced, and it took me about a year to be able to say that to myself, when times were rough.

I decided early on in my marriage, though, that we were not "meant to be together." I noticed that when I thought that about my other boyfriends in the past, it always turned out to be a flop. The first time I met him, I assumed he was "the one" if he was a return missionary and single. That was a failing of my previous high school notion that hooking up with someone would make me happy, but when I got married and took the *real* plunge, I knew I had to find the way to make it through.

A lot of letting go is finding out what you're good at and going for it. I am a pianist. I have played since I was a baby, really. I have a picture where I am sitting in front of a piano with my diaper on, picking at the keys. It is really a good representation of the desire I always had to play. It was really innate. I do not remember never being able to play the piano. That's why it drove me to curiosity, thinking I could

I walked in the back door, and walked to the front of the building, where I stopped to talk to the receptionist.

"Can I help you?"

"Yes, I have a question for you. I am interested in offering my skills as a pianist. I wanted, um, to be able to use them, and I thought maybe you had a use for them." Because I was nervous, I stumbled over my words, "Is there anybody who needs—or, could I speak with the activities director?"

"Oh, that's wonderful! You know, I don't think they need one here, but I'll call over in HALF to see if there is anyone there that could speak with you."

Afterwards

Do you ever think that your life is just a dream? Do you ever think that it will end up being a play in somebody's high school drama class? Or that maybe you will be a famous author and bring a laugh to some mother who is distressed and caught up in the day to day activities of her life?

I have thought of these things for the space of my entire life, and when I left on that day to see some doctors in the far NorthWest Chicago, I realized some of it might happen. It was a beautiful day, and I wanted to be somewhere I could taste the sunshine. I wanted peace, and I lived that day like I would have it, hoping that it would come.

And, I'll tell you, it usually does come, not when you ask for it to. But, like a slow process. And, then, it comes when you are nearly dead from trying and your ends are frayed, and there is no hope in sight. When you give it one last chance, then the answer comes.

A little theatrical. But true. That was a big day for me. I wanted to remember it.

Slowly, I realized something about myself that I had not understood before, and it was during a very important, life-changing event that I found the peace I needed. I found myself in a dimly lighted room, waiting for a prognosis for the condition that has plagued my mind since the first day I missed my father.

I had found myself in my car with a woman I had hardly spoken to a few days earlier, and I did not really want to, since I had found out what was really bothering me. I hold a lot of anger inside towards my mother, because I did not know my father. I had held onto that pain for an entire 10 months of dating, and a year of marriage, before I finally realized that I had to let go of it.

That is where I was when I realized that this was not going to work unless I confronted her about my feelings. We sat a rest stop, and I proceeded to tell her what I felt about my childhood, and that I wished I had known who he was, and at least, heard his voice now and then. She listened intently, and I finished with a resort to peace.

"I want peace in our relationship, mom. I do not want to hold onto the hurt anymore."

She nodded, and I think I ended it with something like, "Well, let's go, I have to pee."

You have to remember here that mom is not totally healed from her past, and even though she did everything she could to prevent me from feeling the same pain, it came. It has been hell trying to get through the pain of losing my father was not the biggest problem in my childhood. However, through the pain, she had been my biggest supporter. I knew that there was a way up, and I was determined to find it. I thought forgiveness would provide that opportunity.

What I found was that testing the waters, trying to talk about the past with her was the most therapeutic thing for me. I never had seen the reality of being a daughter of an alcoholic and a mentally unstable man like I did that day. She and I spoke candidly, and I realized I had hit the nail on the head. Mom did hold back the truth from me, and she did not give me a chance to understand reality because she was afraid herself. It hurt so much. It hurt for so long. I was trying with everything in me to forgive her that day. And, it was certainly a step in the right direction, but it wouldn't be enough to clear the baggage.

When I walked into the rest stop station, I was enthralled to find profane writing on the stalls of the bathroom. I felt like letting go of it, but by the time I left, I could not help but mention to the custodian something about it.

"You would be amazed. I think what the women write are worse than what the men write."

"Really?"

"Oh yeah. It's a wonder what the women write, but I've seen them walking through here. Some of them had on blue jeans and a sweatshirt, with their hair tied back.

They were walking that way, and I said, 'Hey, wait a minute. You're going' the wrong way. Men's restroom is behind you.'

Boy, they turned around and said, 'Who do you think you are?! I'll have you know that I've got breasts!'

That was the last time I tried to tell them where to go. Yeah, it has been pretty crazy."

"I know. I believe there is a lot of crazy stuff going on. It's terrible."

Touching Reality

I walked into church that day with every other possible thing my mind that I could imagine. I was depressed, possibly going to be evicted, and everything was falling apart in front of me. I had had my fair share of the depressing part of reality, and I just wanted to feel whole.

I looked at Josh. He was holding my hand. *What's happened to him? I don't even recognize this man*, I thought. He was more than enough of a hunk, but the fact that he was actually giving me the time of day was amazing.

It all had been so fast. The rush of emotion. The feeling of joy in my heart, I couldn't help but be enthralled by his presence. He was magnificent, even in the face of so much argument and disagreement on *both* our parts. I just knew I had to stick it out if I was going to get anything from our relationship. My survival instincts kicked in. I was a woman with a passionate man. I was passionate. We were both passionate. And, we were going in the totally wrong direction.

I still remember that day we were in the parking lot. I was grieving for the loss of my father. I wanted him so much. I felt the anger well up inside of me. It was like a current of water rushing through me. And it all came up to my throat, and stopped.

Why? Why can't I let go of this feeling? It engulfed me.

I could have resorted then to anything that would have helped. But, I chose to move forward. I was chosen for this time. I believed that.

Again, I came back to reality, here we were after so many agonizing days in our first year, and we were still together. I looked at him, and I smiled. He was beaming. He loved church. It was part of his reason for living. And, I loved it on. Although, I had struggled to realize that during our first year.

That was not the battle going on inside of me. It was not the relationship with God that was the problem. God was on my side. He wanted me to succeed. He was the one who sent me the hands to help me. The friends who never deserted me. The people who loved me, despite my "prickly" exterior. I was hoping for some sort of redemption through the mindfulness exercises I had practiced so much. It always helped, but never enough.

That day, I was looking for a reason behind the chaos. I wanted it to end. Where did it begin? I was back in my hometown and looking for a way out of the madness.

I saw a friend. She passed by with her children.

All grown up, wow, I thought. *She must have a really good head on her shoulders with the way that she takes care of herself and her kids. She always did know how to get what she wanted. And, she never turned back. That's what I need to do.*

This is the girl, you should know, that actually deserted her return missionary for a guy that was in trouble with his morality. She deserted him for that guy? That's what everyone was thinking, when it happened anyways. But, she seemed so happy.

Then I thought, *Oh yeah, I did the same thing.*

I looked back at the person in the mirror and the image of cleavage staring back at me. Today, at least, I was okay. I was alone. Josh was in training for a new job that he worked really hard to get.

I don't remember seeing that before. When did I get to be this? I feel beautiful. I remember when I couldn't even look in the mirror and feel beautiful. I thought that the reason I felt beautiful was because I was a lesbian.

You see, I was a homophobe for a really long time. I used to like thinking like a man. Because I was smart, but really, I didn't have much else in common with the male species. But, they fascinated me because I was smart like them. I had a head on my shoulders. I knew my way around. I could get to where I was going. I wasn't an invalid. Yet, in every thought, every moment, the energy drained from me. One look in the direction of a stranger, I was lost to my innards. And, they were twisted inside and out from seven years on psychiatric therapy.

So, I just cowered from everyone. I thought I could be okay if I just got on the right meds. If I knew how to live without feeling suicidal. I would be able to get up on my feet again. I would be able to try to live again. But, it had been so long since I had felt the light of day without groaning inside when I had to look at myself in the mirror. It was like seeing a reflection that didn't fade. It was always there. Empty. It stared at me with an innocent desire to feel loved. But, I had noticed lately that I glared at myself.

I was miserable. I didn't really know it, though. I was so angry with my stepfather for taking care of me without giving the faith I revered due credit. *How could he not see how it had blessed my life? Am the only one hurting here? Somebody, wake up!*

I screamed inside at every person who ever could have possibly hurt me. I was enraged by the typical human encounters that have cause for distancing. But, instead, I grew angry and I instigated things, and looking back, I was only responding to imagined threats to my ego. I had lost it a long time ago, in a psychologist's office. He was a member of that church, and I dare not say his name now, for he is well aware at this point what he had not considered in giving me the diagnosis that he did.

And, whatever price he must pay for it will be his to inherit in eternity. I have paid mine. And, he must allocate his resources, and make his decisions based on his ability to move forward. I am not alone, however, any longer. And, his diagnosis, though well-intended was wrong, and it was extremely hindering to my psyche, my self confidence, and my ability to believe in myself.

That was really the main problem for me in going to church. I knew my heart was right, but somehow the things I had been force-fed from him caused me so much harm that I would never be the same. And, not to mention, the people that so ardently defended my grandmother, who somehow found her own therapy.

HOwever *her life was much different than mine. And, I was not laying down and dying on this day.*

So, I sat down and listened to the sermon. It was another quiet day for everyone to reflect on the meaning of eternity. And, I was still trying to figure out the meaning of life. *Could somebody please tell me where the exit is? This is making me nervous. I don't even know who I am right now. How could I possibly be attending church to help other people. I am supposed to be on my feet standing with praise for God.* I always felt Mormons were a little too laid back in their testimonies.

But, I listened. I tried really hard to listen, and I tried to pray, until I kept getting messages from God. They came in the form of people who wanted to get to know my husband and I. But, usually they came from my Church, where people are assigned to have service opportunities. And, they were usually assigned to serve me.

I looked up and saw a woman with blonde hair, she was supposed to talk to me, see how I was doing, and offer any help. I wanted to ask her for a ride to the nearest train station, so I could leave the state. But, that didn't happen to be likely since I couldn't buy a ticket, and my work history had been a hardship for me since I started school. I was a very accomplished woman, but nobody's perfect. I was pretty confused about my life.

She reached out to give me a hug, "How are you, Amanda? It's so good to see you."

I glared at her. I was so angry with everyone. If they were to even remotely try to care about me, I was going to push them away. After all, my dad did leave. At least, that's what my mom told me. It was so very difficult to know the truth about people these days, though. The medication they put me on had actually been given to me for the purpose of removing hallucinations, delusions, and psychotic symptoms.

What they did do to help, though, seemed to make me believe everything I wasn't supposed to. I felt like my mom was out of reach. I was alone inside. It was like my whole world was caving in on me. The moment I tried to reach out to any woman. I thought I would lose my sanity just thinking of the last time I saw her beautiful face, lit up with approval. It wasn't easy for me to be around women. MOstly, I felt I had to please them. Otherwise, the world said they were just objects to be desired. I just felt really confused about other women.

I was fine with myself, though. I could be beautiful. But, when I didn't respond to other women with compassion, since I was pretty, most of them looked at me with disdain. I suppose they thought that I was being critical or judgemental in mind. Oh, how very wrong I was to not reach out to them. It was impossible, though, because I was not yet fully developed in my own right as a woman.

I had to detach myself from the idea of losing myself in her. So, I reached out to touch her shoulder. It was so hard to appear happy on the outside, and to be so miserable on the inside. I was gasping for emotional nourishment. It was, however, impossible to receive it. I felt alone, afraid, bewildered, lost, and consequently I just shut down. Every time I was in the room with another woman, I thought I was in competition. I thought I had to recompose myself. I thought I had to let go of something inside. It was my identity.

And, I lost it in a room full of women. Some of them were good women. Others were just waiting for a good man to return to them, after they lost their husband, to their work, to their golfing, their satisfying football parties, and they worked so hard to fulfill their every need.

Well, I'm not like that.

I don't try to fulfill everyone's last need. I don't give up when someone isn't interested in me. I just let them go. And, you know what, I have had a lot of men be interested in me. But, when I start to hold onto them, they seem to let go of me.

And, I've learned something about myself.

I don't really know myself at all.

Because if I were all that needy, wouldn't every woman, in the churches I've been to, have had to see it in me? Wouldn't they have told me to let him go? Wouldn't I have had to push a little harder to please them?

I'm learning that I love men, and I like dating, but I really only loved one man. And, he left me. And, now, I don't have to cling to anyone. He was my dad. And, when he left, I was young, but I still remember that moment.

And, that day, holding my husband's hand in the middle of the room full of faith-seeking men and women reminded me that I needed him.

I needed him. Oh, how I needed him. He was my breath. Like the one I held so close to me, so that nobody could tell how very bad it hurt to be. How if I had taken that breath, the next thought would be a myriad of painful memories, and I would have to scream with agony for the one man in my life that I thought would be mine.

I looked back at my husband, who was going to Sunday School. I tried to breath, but he took it away from me. All that anger, pain, hate, and envy was gone. All that was left was peace, and calm. It was the calm reprise from a thousand moments of hatred and anger. And, he was supposed to be my mate.

How could I desert him now? So, I stayed. I would not sit without anxiety building inside of me. it was funny, I think now, because I didn't feel the anxiety inside of me. I only felt the reality of a drowning sea of emotion swirling inside. I guess I've been anxious my whole life. And, I never really knew it.

I sat with piety, hoping to leave at the next "Amen." But, that didn't happen because I knew I would need those prayers to get through the next week.

So, I prayed while I sat there in a meeting of prayer, that I would know whether or not I was supposed to even be alive. And, surrounded by their prayers, I would make through another day of being me.

Freedom

It was my mother's love that kept me alive for so long. I ached to know her and desired her love. I hoped to keep her close to me. And, the day I died would never be soon enough. It really did hurt that bad to know that I was disappointing her. And, I would wait for someone to make a comment in class and I would raise my hand to contradict. People didn't really take well to it, but I could let it go. I wasn't all that impressed with their abilities to see reality for what it was.

I had done plenty of that.

So, I had had enough of the lies and tricks that people had gotten me into. I had been told I would live forever if I tried to be good the best way I knew how. And, I knew a lot about being good.

But, when I realized that God wanted me to be good and happy, then I questioned my motives and I started to like being alive. Was I really involved in this work of God just so I could become a friend to the others who were like me? Who had pretty hair? Who liked to play the piano? Could I really be happy with one person the rest of my entire living days and then die and be close to them in spirit, inherit eternal lie and still *be happy*?

The answer, to be truthful, was yes. I could. But, it seemed like everyone around me was really absorbed in their cookie making, their decorating, their sewing, their show-watching, and babysitting. I couldn't care less about any of those things. For one, I didn't know if I even wanted kids. And, I couldn't find a job and like it, so much so that I just let them think I gave up. But, none of this was for lack of trying. I was never welcome to those meetings. I was always shown kindness, but I never felt strong by the side of those women.

So, I started to get on my knees and I really started to talk to God.

I tried to ask him questions, and I sometimes just heard those women's doubts inside of me. The same ones I mentioned at the beginning of this chapter. I was losing myself in other people's questions, but my questions were not the same. My questions were about self-worth, happiness, joy, the things that we want to feel in this life. And, most of all, love. Where in the world did *that* come from? I never felt that anymore.

Finally, I think I came to the conclusion that I was not alone, after all, those women never gave up on me. They always called me. And, I realized that I was supposed to be there.

So, when people tell me that they are afraid of something, I just say, DO IT ANYWAY. That's what I did. And, I learned that the things I was afraid of aren't usually what they seem to be.

The love I felt from those women carried me through ten thousand diverse pains. There were ladies who could not have children, women who were old and could not live without friends, women who overscheduled themselves and ignored their own health, and women who would die trying to obtain a professional career.

I felt like, by the end of my stay in that area of the state, and being in that place, I had experienced all of those women's pains. Their sadness, their hopes, their tragedies, and their triumphs. I had gone through it all with them. And, they would, by their own endeavor, learn about me. And, I would in turn be able to let go.

Because I learned to harbor their pain as they did mine. They became my own, and my heart was theirs, while I saw these experiences from the inside. I grew within, while I showed my rough edges, while I allowed their faith to sand those faults from me. I was not suddenly alone. But, I was my own worst enemy.

So, I came up for another breath, and suddenly we pulled into the parking lot at our apartment in the middle of metropolitan chaos, while the hot summer sun beat down and baked our skin, I thought about why I was going to church, while the inside of me was growing from the sun's bright and shining rays.

It was a gift from God just to be alive.